SHADOWS

A Trinity of Plays by J. M. Synge and W. B. Yeats

J. M. SYNGE

RIDERS TO THE SEA
THE SHADOW OF THE GLEN

W. B. YEATS

PURGATORY

OBERON BOOKS
LONDON

This edition published in 1998 by Oberon Books Ltd.,
(incorporating Absolute Classics),
521 Caledonian Road,
London N7 9RH.
Tel: 0171 607 3637 / Fax: 0171 607 3629

British Library Cataloguing-in-Publication Data
A Catalogue record for this book is available from the British Library.

ISBN 1 84002 027 X

Cover photograph: Paul Rider

Cover design: Andrzej Klimowski

Typography: Richard Doust

Printed in Great Britain by Arrowhead Books Ltd., Reading.

CONTENTS

INTRODUCTION

The Living and the Dead: Synge and Yeats

by Declan Kiberd

A suitable subtitle for each of these three plays might be 'The Undead' (and it may be no coincidence that the author of *Dracula* was an Irishman). Each play is devoted to the proposition that life as we know it is never enough and that to die is to be set free of life rather than simply deprived of it.

For the Irish peasantry, in whose world the plays are set in the earlier decades of the 20th century, the borderline between the living and dead was vague indeed. Spirits often returned to stake an outstanding claim, sometimes taking one of the living back with them to 'the far side'. On other occasions, the living might simply converse with the souls of those long dead. In the national politics of the period a similar mentality prevailed: figures from the Home Ruler Parnell to the hunger-striker MacSwiney seemed to exercise even more influence in death than they had ever managed to achieve in life. In an Irish democracy the dead are always recognised to have rights, if not actual votes.

John Millington Synge (1871–1909) was the first great playwright of the national dramatic movement. His most famous work, *The Playboy of the Western World* provoked riots on its first production at the Abbey Theatre in 1907, but its anti-heroic conception of rural life had been anticipated, in a more tragic key, by *Riders to the Sea* (1903), a work which some consider the most perfect one-act play in the English language.

Though *Riders* runs for less than half an hour, it is in the fullest sense of the word a tragedy: the old woman Maurya is shown to be not only a pathetic victim of fate but also an author of her own misfortune. Audiences at the Abbey Theatre, patriotic and well-versed in Gaelic folklore, would have seen in her failure to bless her departing son Bartley a painful violation of a most ancient code. To withhold such a blessing was, in effect, to condemn a traveller to bad luck, even death. Maurya's silence may have been a desperate gamble, sustained in hopes that her son would recognise what feelings of unutterable love prompted her objection to his journey. Or perhaps hers was the silence of an exhausted woman, numbed by years of suffering in the course of which she had lost her husband and her other sons to the sea.

Synge himself, when he talked with the fishermen of Aran, felt that they were already under a sentence of death: and he found the island women tortured by the possibility that they would rear children only to lose them to sea or emigrant-ship. Hence their need to keep their maternal feelings in perpetual check. Maurya *may* be concealing a similar tenderness from Bartley, but her daughters do not think so, noting that she shed more tears for another lost son, Michael. Whatever the truth of all this, one thing is very clear: Maurya can really only express the full scope of her feelings for her children when they are dead. With the living, she can often seem callous, as when she tells her daughters at the end 'they're all gone now', in tones which suggest that the two women still by her side just do not count.

If Maurya contributed to the catastrophe by sending an unblessed Bartley to a fatal encounter with the spirit of the dead Michael, she does in those final moments over his recovered body manage to give the blessing which earlier had been refused. Abbey audiences would have understood just how symbolic her every action (hoping to repair her error by pursuing Bartley with the bread of life) and inaction were (allowing the fire, which symbolised life, to go out).

On stage, every prop is a symbol. The cup which Maurya turns over at the close must be taken out of circulation as a hygienic measure, lest its dead owner return to claim its next user (for, after all, Michael had come back from the dead to claim the brother who dared to wear his shirt): but the overturning of a cup which recently contained holy water is also Maurya's way of showing how ineffectual the Catholic religion has been in its perennial contest with the pagan force of the sea. That sea is shown invading the little cottage in the salt-water which drips from the sail which holds the body of the drowned man.

The dead and living share (despite folk taboos) the same utensils, the same clothes, even the same limited number of phrases. Words once used by Maurya are soon recycled by her younger daughter Nora, who just minutes earlier had herself complained of such repetition from a woman 'with one thing and she saying it over'. In such a world of drastic limitation, the death of Bartley may be less radical a breach than the earlier moment which saw a mother unable to bless a son. Yet at the close Maurya transcends all thoughts of self and finds it possible to bless not alone Bartley but every soul left living in the world. By a miraculous paradox, at the very end of her life she develops, perhaps for the first time, a powerful sense of the future *and* an utterly unexpected capacity to locate her own suffering in a wider pattern of moral significance. This Lear-like epiphany explains her refusal to cry: she has just experienced an inner vision, yet the attendant irony is that her two daughters, quite unaware of this transformation, conclude that she has lost all capacity for feeling.

By way of contrast with all that intensity, *The Shadow of the Glen* (1903) is a mischievous farce: yet central to it also is the sense that the dead Patch Darcy is more alive to Nora Burke than any living man. The play begins as a 'wake' for Nora's recently-deceased husband Dan. Although praise of the dead was the main conversational agenda on such occasions, all the plaudits go to the virile Patch rather than the husband who, Nora tells a visiting Tramp, was always cold every day 'and every night, stranger'.

Dan Burke is shamming death in order to test his wife's fidelity, but in a deeper sense his act hints at a kind of truth, for he is one of the living dead. Patch, though long buried, lives on in the spirit of a bored housewife and homeless tramp who, in the end, would prefer to live intensely for a limited time, risking early death, than settle for a life of dull routine and deathly evasion.

Water-imagery is important here too. The rain outside lashes down and may shorten their lives out in the natural world, but it also nourishes life, whereas inside the cottage all is drouth and dryness, the dryness of death. Nora Burke learns that there is no safety from the shadow of death in a domestic world and so, like the more famous Nora of Ibsen, she walks out through the door – but she is not alone, having left in the company of a man whose name she doesn't even know. His air of mystery and gift of language are enough.

The Tramp's honeyed words may strike old Dan as 'blathering', but to Nora they are fine 'talk' (and the distinction is crucial). If old Dan's sentences are filled with barren repetitions, the Tramp's are filled with participles which teach this woman, perhaps for the first time in her life, how to live in the present tense. A feeling for the possibilities of language becomes the test of moral potential in Synge's plays and those who lack it condemn themselves out of their own mouths, for the Abbey was above all a poet's theatre.

The Shadow of the Glen is Synge's challenge to time and to decay, a challenge composed by an artist who knew himself to be a sick, possibly doomed, man. As in *Riders to the Sea*, he was very careful to get the details of folk belief exactly right: the tramp's insistence on tobacco and whiskey is part of 'wake' ritual, as is the notion that at least one person must always sit by the dead body, keeping company with the soul as it passes out of it and over into the other world.

The poet William Butler Yeats (1865–1939) was the founder and major theorist of the Irish National Theatre Society. He outlived Synge by three decades, in the course of which he produced many experimental dramas, including a cycle devoted to the Celtic hero Cuchulain (as a reworking of Shakespeare's own national epic of Tudor plays). Yeats's last play *Purgatory* (1939), limited in setting to a bare tree, a ruined landscape and two characters speaking a bleak, jagged poetry, seems to anticipate the drama of Samuel Beckett, but it also looks back to that ancient Irish (and cabbalistic) tradition which holds that the remorseful dead must return to reenact their painful lives until their sins have all been expiated. Yeats sees this world itself as purgatorial, the zone to which the unhappy dead must come back.

His play analyses the decline of the great Anglo-Irish houses: and he is honest enough to admit that the decline came more from within than without, as the aristocracy fell to a combination of fast women and slow horses rather than to republican attack. By 1939 many of the Big House shells were being huckstered off to tradesmen of the new state and summarily razed: and so, as an admirer of aristocracy, Yeats cannot but find their loss 'a capital offence'.

Deeper than this, however, is his notion of a past which must eternally return and from which even the most violent person would pray to be delivered. In the attempt to purge their sin, the characters merely repeat it, hoping against hope that each attempt will be the last. They are literally commemorating themselves to death, but they have no choice, for the alternative is unthinkable – to bring the work of the dead to nothing. The members of a once-great family are punished not just for their sins but by their sins: and yet their trust is that sooner or later the talking cure, the reenactment, will finally purge. Though they learn from history, they are nonetheless doomed to repeat it.

Declan Kiberd
Dublin, 1998

Director's Note

In addition to a number of landmark plays of twentieth century drama, one of the legacies of the Abbey Theatre's early years is a vast repertoire of one-act plays. These short plays sit around gathering dust like antiques which no one seems quite sure what to do with any more. They have lost their performance context and, not surprisingly, plays like *The Playboy of the Western World* or Sean O'Casey's *Dublin Trilogy* are revived most frequently, for better or worse epitomising that period of Irish theatre.

Apart from being frequently referred to in hushed tones as 'masterpieces', the three plays published in this volume are unified by a thematic thread – death – or more specifically the refusal of the dead to leave the living alone. Performing the three together with a company of actors doubling roles offered rich possibilities. The plays complement and illuminate each other but, more interestingly, the individual, haunting spirit of each one echoes in the other two.

John Crowley

Shadows, A Trinity of Plays by J. M. Synge and W. B. Yeats was first performed by the Royal Shakespeare Company at The Other Place, Stratford-upon-Avon, on 18 February 1998. The cast, in order of appearance, was as follows:

Riders to the Sea by J. M. Synge

Cathleen   *Mairead McKinley*
Nora   *Aislinn Mangan*
Maurya   *Stella McCusker*
Bartley   *Stephen Kennedy*
Neighbour   *Lalor Roddy*
Neighbour   *Owen Sharpe*

The Shadow of the Glen by J. M. Synge

Nora   *Mairead McKinley*
Tramp   *Stephen Kennedy*
Dan   *Lalor Roddy*
Michael   *Owen Sharpe*

Purgatory by W. B. Yeats

Old Man   *Lalor Roddy*
Boy   *Owen Sharpe*

Director   *John Crowley*
Designer   *Angela Davies*
Lighting   *Tina McHugh*
Music   *Tommy Hayes*
Sound   *Andrea J. Cox*
Company voice work   *Lyn Darnley and Andrew Wade*
Production Manager   *Mark Graham*
Costume Supervisor   *Jenny Alden*

Stage Manager   *Katie Vine*
Deputy Stage Manager   *Liz Burton*
Assistant Stage Manager   *Elizabeth Frank*

Musicians
Uileann pipes/whistles   *Martin Furey*
Bodhran/bones   *James Jones*

RIDERS TO THE SEA

A play in one act

by J. M. Synge

PERSONS IN THE PLAY

MAURYA, an old woman

BARTLEY, her son

CATHLEEN, her daughter

NORA, a younger daughter

MEN AND WOMEN

SCENE

An Island off the West of Ireland.

Cottage kitchen, with nets, oil-skins, spinning wheel, some new boards standing by the wall, etc. CATHLEEN, a girl of about twenty, finishes kneading a cake, and puts it down in the pot-oven by the fire; then wipes her hands, and begins to spin at the wheel. NORA, a young girl, puts her head in at the door.

NORA (*in a low voice*): Where is she?

CATHLEEN: She's lying down, God help her, and maybe sleeping, if she's able.

(NORA comes in softly, and takes a bundle from under her shawl.)

CATHLEEN (*Spinning the wheel rapidly*): What is it you have?

NORA: The young priest is after bringing them. It's a shirt and a plain stocking were got off a drowned man in Donegal.

(CATHLEEN stops her wheel with a sudden movement, and leans out to listen.)

NORA: We're to find out if it's Michael's they are, some time herself will be down looking by the sea.

CATHLEEN: How would they be Michael's, Nora. How would he go the length of that way to the far north?

NORA: The young priest says he's known the like of it. "If it's Michael's they are," says he, "you can tell herself he's got a clean burial by the grace of God, and if they're not his, let no one say a word about them, for she'll be getting her death," says he, "with crying and lamenting."

(*The door which NORA half closed behind her is blown open by a gust of wind.*)

CATHLEEN (*Looking out anxiously*): Did you ask him would he stop Bartley going this day with the horses to the Galway fair?

NORA: "I won't stop him," says he, "but let you not be afraid. Herself does be saying prayers half through the night, and the Almighty God won't leave her destitute," says he, "with no son living."

CATHLEEN: Is the sea bad by the white rocks, Nora?

NORA: Middling bad, God help us. There's a great roaring in the west, and it's worse it'll be getting when the tide's turned to the wind. (*She goes over to the table with the bundle.*) Shall I open it now?

CATHLEEN: Maybe she'd wake up on us, and come in before we'd done (*coming to the table*). It's a long time we'll be, and the two of us crying.

NORA (*Goes to the inner door and listens*): She's moving about on the bed. She'll be coming in a minute.

CATHLEEN: Give me the ladder, and I'll put them up in the turf-loft, the way she won't know of them at all, and maybe when the tide turns she'll be going down to see would he be floating from the east.

(*They put the ladder against the gable of the chimney; CATHLEEN goes up a few steps and hides the bundle in the turf-loft. MAURYA comes from the inner room.*)

MAURYA (*Looking up at CATHLEEN and speaking querulously*): Isn't it turf enough you have for this day and evening?

CATHLEEN: There's a cake baking at the fire for a short space (*throwing down the turf*), and Bartley will want it when the tide turns if he goes to Connemara.

(*NORA picks up the turf and puts it round the pot-oven.*)

MAURYA (*Sitting down on a stool at the fire*): He won't go this day with the wind rising from the south and west. He won't go this day, for the young priest will stop him surely.

NORA: He'll not stop him, mother, and I heard Eamon Simon and Stephen Pheety and Colum Shawn saying he would go.

MAURYA: Where is he itself?

NORA: He went down to see would there be another boat sailing in the week, and I'm thinking it won't be long till he's here now, for the tide's turning at the green head, and the hooker's tacking from the east.

CATHLEEN: I hear some one passing the big stones.

NORA (*Looking out*): He's coming now, and he in a hurry.

BARTLEY (*Comes in and looks round the room; speaking sadly and quietly*): Where is the bit of new rope, Cathleen, was bought in Connemara?

CATHLEEN (*coming down*): Give it to him, Nora; it's on a nail by the white boards. I hung it up this morning, for the pig with the black feet was eating it.

NORA (*Giving him a rope*): Is that it, Bartley?

MAURYA (*As before*): You'd do right to leave that rope, Bartley, hanging by the boards. (*BARTLEY takes the rope.*) It will be wanting in this place, I'm telling you, if Michael is washed up tomorrow morning, or the next morning, or any morning in the week, for it's a deep grave we'll make him by the grace of God.

BARTLEY (*Beginning to work with the rope*): I've no halter the way I can ride down on the mare, and I must go now quickly. This is the one boat going for two weeks or beyond it, and the fair will be a good fair for horses I heard them saying below.

MAURYA: It's a hard thing they'll be saying below if the body is washed up and there's no man in it to make the coffin, and I after giving a big price for the finest white boards you'd find in Connemara. (*She looks round at the boards.*)

BARTLEY: How would it be washed up, and we after looking each day for nine days, and a strong wind blowing a while back from the west and south?

MAURYA: If it isn't found itself, that wind is raising the sea, and there was a star up against the moon, and it rising in the night. If it was a hundred horses, or a thousand horses you had itself, what is the price of a thousand horses against a son where there is one son only?

BARTLEY (*Working at the halter, to CATHLEEN*): Let you go down each day, and see the sheep aren't jumping in on the rye, and if the jobber comes you can sell the pig with the black feet if there is a good price going.

MAURYA: How would the like of her get a good price for a pig?

BARTLEY (*To CATHLEEN*): If the west wind holds with the last bit of the moon let you and Nora get up weed enough for another cock for the kelp. It's hard set we'll be from this day with no one in it but one man to work.

MAURYA: It's hard set we'll be surely the day you're drown'd with the rest. What way will I live and the girls with me, and I an old woman looking for the grave?

(*BARTLEY lays down the halter, takes off his old coat, and puts on a newer one of the same flannel.*)

BARTLEY (*To NORA*): Is she coming to the pier?

NORA (*Looking out*): She's passing the green head and letting fall her sails.

BARTLEY (*Getting his purse and tobacco*): I'll have half an hour to go down, and you'll see me coming again in two days, or in three days, or maybe in four days if the wind is bad.

19

MAURYA (*Turning round to the fire, and putting her shawl over her head*): Isn't it a hard and cruel man won't hear a word from an old woman, and she holding him from the sea?

CATHLEEN: It's the life of a young man to be going on the sea, and who would listen to an old woman with one thing and she saying it over?

BARTLEY (*Taking the halter*): I must go quickly. I'll ride down on the red mare, and the grey pony'll run behind me... The blessing of God on you. (*He goes out.*)

MAURYA (*Crying out as he is in the doorway*): He's gone now, God spare us, and we'll not see him again. He's gone now, and when the black night is falling I'll have no son left me in the world.

CATHLEEN: Why wouldn't you give him your blessing and he looking round in the door? Isn't it sorrow enough is on every one in this house without your sending him out with an unlucky word behind him, and a hard word in his ear?

(*MAURYA takes up the tongs and begins raking the fire aimlessly without looking round.*)

NORA (*Turning towards her*): You're taking away the turf from the cake.

CATHLEEN (*Crying out*): The Son of God forgive us, Nora, we're after forgetting his bit of bread. (*She comes over to the fire.*)

NORA: And it's destroyed he'll be going till dark night, and he after eating nothing since the sun went up.

CATHLEEN (*Turning the cake out of the oven*): It's destroyed he'll be, surely. There's no sense left on any person in a house where an old woman will be talking forever.

(*MAURYA sways herself on her stool.*)

CATHLEEN (*Cutting off some of the bread and rolling it in a cloth; to MAURYA*): Let you go down now to the spring well and give him this and he passing. You'll see him then and the dark word will be broken, and you can say "God speed you," the way he'll be easy in his mind.

MAURYA (*Taking the bread*): Will I be in it as soon as himself?

CATHLEEN: If you go now quickly.

MAURYA (*Standing up unsteadily*): It's hard set I am to walk.

CATHLEEN (*Looking at her anxiously*): Give her the stick, Nora, or maybe she'll slip on the big stones.

NORA: What stick?

CATHLEEN: The stick Michael brought her from Connemara.

MAURYA (*Taking a stick NORA gives her*): In the big world the old people do be leaving things after them for their sons and children, but in this place it is the young men do be leaving things behind for them that do be old. (*She goes out slowly.*)

(*NORA goes over to the ladder.*)

CATHLEEN: Wait, Nora, maybe she'd turn back quickly. She's that sorry, God help her, you wouldn't know the thing she'd do.

NORA: Is she gone round by the bush?

CATHLEEN (*Looking out*): She's gone now. Throw it down quickly, for the Lord knows when she'll be out of it again.

NORA (*Getting the bundle from the loft*): The young priest said he'd be passing tomorrow, and we might go down and speak to him below if it's Michael's they are surely.

CATHLEEN (*Taking the bundle from NORA*): Did he say what way they were found?

NORA (*Coming down*): "There were two men," says he, "and they rowing round with poteen before the cocks crowed, and the oar of one of them caught the body, and they passing the black cliffs of the north."

CATHLEEN (*Trying to open the bundle*): Give me a knife, Nora, the string's perished with the salt water, and there's a black knot on it you wouldn't loosen in a week.

NORA (*Giving her a knife*): I've heard tell it was a long way to Donegal.

CATHLEEN (*Cutting the string*): It is surely. There was a man in here a while ago – the man sold us that knife – and he said if you set off walking from the rocks beyond, it would be in seven days you'd be in Donegal.

NORA: And what time would a man take, and he floating?

(*CATHLEEN opens the bundle and takes out a bit of a shirt and a stocking. They look at them eagerly.*)

CATHLEEN (*In a low voice*): The Lord spare us, Nora! Isn't it a queer hard thing to say if it's his they are surely?

NORA: I'll get his shirt off the hook the way we can put the one flannel on the other. (*She looks through some clothes hanging in the corner.*) It's not with them, Cathleen, and where will it be?

CATHLEEN: I'm thinking Bartley put it on him in the morning, for his own shirt was heavy with the salt in it. (*Pointing to the corner.*) There's a bit of the sleeve was of the same stuff. Give me that and it will do.

(*NORA brings it to her and they compare the flannel.*)

CATHLEEN: It's the same stuff, Nora; but if it is itself aren't there great rolls of it in the shops of Galway, and isn't it many another man may have a shirt of it as well as Michael himself?

NORA (*Who has taken up the stocking and counted the stitches, crying out*): It's Michael, Cathleen, it's Michael; God spare his soul, and what will herself say when she hears this story, and Bartley on the sea?

CATHLEEN (*Taking the stocking*): It's a plain stocking.

NORA: It's the second one of the third pair I knitted, and I put up three score stitches, and I dropped four of them.

CATHLEEN (*Counts the stitches*): It's that number is in it. (*Crying out*) Ah, Nora, isn't it a bitter thing to think of him floating that way to the far north, and no one to keen him but the black hags that do be flying on the sea?

NORA (*Swinging herself round and throwing out her arms on the clothes*): And isn't it a pitiful thing when there is nothing left of a man who was a great rower and fisher, but a bit of an old shirt and a plain stocking?

CATHLEEN (*After an instant*): Tell me is herself coming, Nora? I hear a little sound on the path.

NORA (*Looking out*): She is, Cathleen. She's coming up to the door.

CATHLEEN: Put these things away before she'll come in. Maybe it's easier she'll be after giving her blessing to Bartley, and we won't let on we've heard anything the time he's on the sea.

NORA (*Helping CATHLEEN to close the bundle*): We'll put them here in the corner.

(*They put them into a hole in the chimney corner. CATHLEEN goes back to the spinning-wheel.*)

NORA: Will she see it was crying I was?

CATHLEEN: Keep your back to the door the way the light'll not be on you.

(*NORA sits down at the chimney corner, with her back to the door. MAURYA comes in very slowly, without looking at the girls, and goes over to her stool at the other side of the fire. The cloth with the bread is still in her hand. The girls look at each other, and NORA points to the bundle of bread.*)

CATHLEEN (*After spinning for a moment*): You didn't give him his bit of bread?

(*MAURYA begins to keen softly, without turning round.*)

CATHLEEN: Did you see him riding down?

(*MAURYA goes on keening.*)

CATHLEEN (*A little impatiently*): God forgive you; isn't it a better thing to raise your voice and tell what you seen, than to be making lamentation for a thing that's done? Did you see Bartley, I'm saying to you.

MAURYA (*With a weak voice*): My heart's broken from this day.

CATHLEEN (*As before*): Did you see Bartley?

MAURYA: I seen the fearfullest thing.

CATHLEEN (*Leaves her wheel and looks out*): God forgive you; he's riding the mare now over the green head, and the grey pony behind him.

MAURYA (*Starts, so that her shawl falls back from her head and shows her white tossed hair. With a frightened voice*): The grey pony behind him...

CATHLEEN (*Coming to the fire*): What is it ails you, at all?

MAURYA (*Speaking very slowly*): I've seen the fearfullest thing any person has seen, since the day Bride Dara seen the dead man with the child in his arms.

CATHLEEN and NORA: Uah.

(*They crouch down in front of the old woman at the fire.*)

NORA: Tell us what it is you seen.

MAURYA: I went down to the spring well, and I stood there saying a prayer to myself. Then Bartley came along, and he riding on the red mare with the grey pony behind him.

(*She puts up her hands, as if to hide something from her eyes.*)

The Son of God spare us, Nora.

CATHLEEN: What is it you seen?

MAURYA: I seen Michael himself.

CATHLEEN (*Speaking softly*): You did not, mother; it wasn't Michael you seen, for his body is after being found in the far north, and he's got a clean burial by the grace of God.

MAURYA (*A little defiantly*): I'm after seeing him this day, and he riding and galloping. Bartley came first on the red mare; and I tried to say "God speed you," but something choked the words in my throat. He went by quickly; and "the blessing of God on you," says he, and I could say nothing. I look up then, and I crying, at the grey pony, and there was Michael upon it – with fine clothes on him, and new shoes on his feet.

CATHLEEN (*Begins to keen*): It's destroyed we are from this day. It's destroyed, surely.

NORA: Didn't the young priest say the Almighty God won't leave her destitute with no son living?

MAURYA (*In a low voice, but clearly*): It's little the like of him knows of the sea... Bartley will be lost now, and let you call in Eamon and make me a good coffin out of the white boards, for I won't live after them. I've had a husband, and a husband's father, and six sons in this house – six fine men, though it was a hard birth I had with every one of them and they coming to the world – and some of them were found and some of them were not found, but they're gone now the lot of them... There were Stephen, and Shawn, were lost in the great wind, and found after in the Bay of Gregory of the Golden Mouth, and carried up the two of them on one plank, and in by that door.

(*She pauses for a moment; the girls start as if they heard something through the door that is half open behind them.*)

NORA (*In a whisper*): Did you hear that, Cathleen? Did you hear a noise in the north-east?

CATHLEEN (*in a whisper*): There's some one after crying out by the seashore.

MAURYA (*Continues without hearing anything*): There was Sheamus and his father, and his own father again, were lost in a dark night, and not a stick or sign was seen of them when the sun went up. There was Patch after was drowned out of a curagh that turned over. I was sitting here with Bartley, and he a baby, lying on my two knees, and I seen two women, and three women, and four women coming in, and they crossing themselves, and not saying a word. I looked out then, and there were men coming after them, and they holding a thing in the half of a red sail, and water dripping out of it — it was a dry day, Nora — and leaving a track to the door.

(*She pauses again with her hand stretched out towards the door. It opens softly and old women begin to come in, crossing themselves on the threshold, and kneeling down in front of the stage with red petticoats over their heads.*)

MAURYA (*Half in a dream, to CATHLEEN*): Is it Patch, or Michael, or what is it at all?

CATHLEEN: Michael is after being found in the far north, and when he is found there how could he be here in this place?

MAURYA: There does be a power of young men floating round in the sea, and what way would they know if it was Michael they had, or another man like him, for when a man is nine days in the sea, and the wind blowing, it's hard set his own mother would be to say what man was in it.

CATHLEEN: It's Michael, God spare him, for they're after sending us a bit of his clothes from the far north.

(*She reaches out and hands MAURYA the clothes that belonged to Michael. MAURYA stands up slowly, and takes them in her hands. NORA looks out.*)

NORA: They're carrying a thing among them and there's water dripping out of it and leaving a track by the big stones.

CATHLEEN (*in a whisper to the women who have come in*): Is it Bartley it is?

(*Two younger women come in and pull out the table. The men carry in the body of BARTLEY, laid on a plank, with a bit of a sail over it, and lay it on the table.*)

THE OLD MAN:[1] It is surely, God rest his soul.

CATHLEEN (*To the man, as he is doing so*): What way was he drowned?

THE OLD MAN: The grey pony knocked him over into the sea, and he was washed out where there is a great surf on the white rocks.

(*MAURYA has gone over and knelt down at the head of the table. The women are keening softly and swaying themselves with a slow movement. CATHLEEN and NORA kneel at the other end of the table. The men kneel near the door.*)

MAURYA (*Raising her head and speaking as if she did not see the people around her*): They're all gone now, and there isn't anything more the sea can do to me... I'll have no call now to be up crying and praying when the wind breaks from the south, and you can hear the surf is in the east, and the surf is in the west, making a great stir with the two noises, and they hitting one on the other. I'll have no call now to be going down and getting Holy Water in the dark nights after Samhain, and I won't care what way the sea is when the other women will be keening. (*To NORA*) Give me the Holy Water, Nora, there's a small sup still on the dresser.

1: One of the old women in the original published version.

(*NORA gives it to her. MAURYA drops Michael's clothes across BARTLEY's feet, and sprinkles the holy Water over him.*)

... It isn't that I haven't prayed for you, Bartley, to the Almighty God. It isn't that I haven't said prayers in the dark night till you wouldn't know what I'd be saying; but it's a great rest I'll have now, and it's time surely. It's a great rest I'll have now, and great sleeping in the long nights after Samhain, if it's only a bit of wet flour we do have to eat, and maybe a fish that would be stinking.

(*She kneels down again, crossing herself, and saying prayers under her breath.*)

CATHLEEN (*To the old man kneeling near her*): Maybe yourself and Eamon would make a coffin when the sun rises. We have fine white boards herself bought, God help her, thinking Michael would be found, and I have a new cake you can eat while you'll be working.

THE OLD MAN (*Looking at the boards*): Are there nails with them?

CATHLEEN: There are not, Colum; we didn't think of the nails.

THE OLD MAN: It's a great wonder she wouldn't think of the nails, and all the coffins she's seen made already.

CATHLEEN: It's getting old she is, and broken.

(*MAURYA stands up again very slowly and spreads out the pieces of Michael's clothes beside the body, sprinkling them with the last of the Holy Water.*)

NORA (*In a whisper to CATHLEEN*): She's quiet now and easy; but the day Michael was drowned you could hear her crying out from this to the spring well. It's fonder she was of Michael, and would any one have thought that?

CATHLEEN (*Slowly and clearly*): An old woman will soon be tired with anything she will do, and isn't it nine days herself is after crying, and keening, and making great sorrow in the house?

MAURYA (*Puts the empty cup mouth downwards on the table, and lays her hands together on BARTLEY's feet*): Theyre all together this time, and the end is come. may the Almighty God have mercy on Bartley's soul, and on Michael's soul, and on the souls of Sheamus and Patch, and Stephen and Shawn (*Bending her head*)... and may He have mercy on my soul, Nora, and on the soul of everyone is left living in the world. (*She pauses, and the keen rises a little more loudly from the women, then sinks away. Continuing.*) Michael has a clean burial in the far north, by the grace of the Almighty God. Bartley will have a fine coffin out of the white boards, and a deep grave surely... What more can we want than that?... No man at all can be living for ever, and we must be satisfied. ·

(*She kneels down again and the curtain falls slowly.*)

CURTAIN

THE SHADOW OF THE GLEN

A play in one act

by J. M. Synge

PERSONS IN THE PLAY

DAN BURKE, farmer and herd

NORA BURKE, his wife

MICHAEL DARA, a young herd

A TRAMP

SCENE

*The last cottage at the head of a long glen
in County Wicklow.*

*Cottage kitchen; turf fire on the right; a bed near it
against the wall with a body lying on it covered with a
sheet. A door is at the other end of the room, with a low
table near it, and stools, or wooden chairs. There are a
couple of glasses on the table, and a bottle of whiskey, as
if for a wake, with two cups, a tea-pot, and a home-
made cake. There is another small door near the bed.
NORA BURKE is moving about the room, settling a
few things and lighting candles on the table, looking
now and then at the bed with an uneasy look. Someone
knocks softly at the door on the left. She takes up a
stocking with money from the table and puts it in her
pocket. Then she opens the door.*

TRAMP (*Outside*): Good evening to you, lady of the
house.

NORA: Good evening kindly, stranger, it's a wild
night, God help you, to be out in the rain falling.

TRAMP: It is surely, and I walking to Brittas from the
Aughrim fair.

NORA: Is it walking on your feet, stranger?

TRAMP: On my two feet, lady of the house, and when
I saw the light below I thought maybe if you'd a sup
of new milk and a quiet decent corner where a man
could sleep... (*He looks in past her and sees the body on
the bed.*) The Lord have mercy on us all!

NORA: It doesn't matter any way, stranger, come in out of the rain.

TRAMP (*Coming in slowly and going towards the bed*): Is it departed he is?

NORA: It is, stranger. He's after dying on me, God forgive him, and there I am now with a hundred sheep beyond on the hills, and no turf drawn for the winter.

TRAMP (*Looking closely at the body*): It's a queer look is on him for a man that's dead.

NORA (*Half-humorously*): He was always queer, stranger, and I suppose them that's queer and they living men will be queer bodies after.

TRAMP: Isn't it a great wonder you're letting him lie there, and he not tidied, or laid out itself?

NORA (*Coming to the bed*): I was afeard, stranger, for he put a black curse on me this morning if I'd touch his body the time he'd die sudden, or let anyone touch it except his sister only, and it's ten miles away she lives, in the big glen over the hill.

TRAMP (*Looking at her and nodding slowly*): It's a queer story he wouldn't let his own wife touch him, and he dying quiet in his bed.

NORA: He was an old man, and an odd man, stranger, and it's always up on the hills he was, thinking thoughts in the dark mist. (*She pulls back a bit more of the sheet.*) Lay your hand on him now, and tell me if it's cold he is surely.

TRAMP: Is it getting the curse on me you'd be, woman of the house? I wouldn't lay my hand on him for the Lough Nahanagan and it filled with gold.

NORA (*Looking uneasily at the body*): Maybe cold would be no sign of death with the like of him, for he was always cold, every day since I knew him, – and every night, stranger – (*She comes away from the bed*); but I'm thinking it's dead he is surely, for he's complaining a while back of a pain in his heart, and this morning, the time he was going off the Brittas for three days or four, he was taken with a sharp turn. Then he went into his bed and he was saying it was destroyed he was, the time the shadow was going up through the glen, and when the sun set on the bog beyond he made a great lep, and let a great cry out of him, and stiffened himself out the like of a dead sheep.

TRAMP (*Crosses himself*): God rest his soul.

NORA (*Pouring him out a glass of whiskey*): Maybe that would do you better than the milk of the sweetest cow in County Wicklow.

TRAMP: The Almighty God reward you, and may it be to your good health. (*He drinks.*)

NORA (*Giving him a pipe and tobacco from the table*): I've no pipes saving his own, stranger, but they're sweet pipes to smoke.

TRAMP: Thank you kindly, lady of the house.

NORA: Sit down now, stranger, and be taking your rest.

37

TRAMP (*Filling a pipe and looking about the room*): I've walked a great way through the world, lady of the house, and seen great wonders, but I never seen a wake till the day with fine spirits, and good tobacco, and the best of pipes, and no one to taste them but a woman only.

NORA: Didn't you hear me say it was only after dying on me he was when the sun went down, and how would I go out into the glen and tell the neighbours and I a lone woman with no house near me?

TRAMP (*Drinking*): There's no offence, lady of the house?

NORA: No offence in life, stranger. How would the like of you passing in the dark night know the lonesome way I was with no house near me at all?

TRAMP (*Sitting down*): I knew rightly. (*He lights his pipe so that there is a sharp light beneath his haggard face.*) And I was thinking, and I coming in through the door, that it's many a lone woman would be afeard of the like of me in the dark night, in a place wouldn't be as lonesome as this place, where there aren't two living souls would see the little light you have shining from the glass.

NORA (*slowly*): I'm thinking many would be afeard, but I never knew what way I'd be afeard of beggar or bishop or any man of you at all. (*She looks towards the window and lowers her voice.*) It's other things than the like of you, stranger, would make a person afeard.

TRAMP (*Looking round with a half-smile*): It is surely, God help us all!

NORA (*Looking at him for a moment with curiosity*):
You're saying that, stranger, as if you were easy
afeard.

TRAMP (*Speaking mournfully*): Is it myself, lady of the
house, that does be walking round in the long
nights, and crossing the hills when the fog is on
them, the time a little stick would seem as big as
your arm, and a rabbit as big as a bay horse, and a
stack of turf as big as a towering church in the city
of Dublin? If myself was easily afeard, I'm telling
you, it's long ago I'd have been locked into the
Richmond Asylum, or maybe have run up into the
back hills with nothing on me but an old shirt, and
been eaten with crows the like of Patch Darcy –
the Lord have mercy on him – in the year that's
gone.

NORA (*With interest*): You knew Darcy?

TRAMP: Wasn't I the last one heard his living voice
in the whole world?

NORA: There were great stories of what was heard at
that time, but would anyone believe the things they
do be saying in the glen?

TRAMP: It was no lie, lady of the house... I was
passing below on a dark night the like of this night,
and the sheep were lying under the ditch and every
one of them coughing, and choking, like an old
man, with the great rain and the fog... Then I heard
a thing talking – queer talk, you wouldn't believe
at all, and you out of your dreams – "Merciful
God," says I, "if I begin hearing the like of that
voice out of the thick mist, I'm destroyed surely."

Then I run, and I run, and I run, till I was below in Rathvanna. I got drunk that night, I got drunk in the morning, and drunk the day after, – I was coming from the races beyond – and the third day they found Darcy... Then I knew it was himself I was after hearing, and I wasn't afeard any more.

NORA (*Speaking mournfully and slowly*): God spare Darcy, he'd always look in here and he passing up or passing down, and it's very lonesome I was after him a long while (*She looks over at the bed and lowers her voice, speaking very clearly*), and then I got happy again – if it's ever happy we are, stranger – for I got used to being lonesome. (*A short pause; then she stands up.*) Was there anyone on the last bit of the road, stranger, and you coming from Aughrim?

TRAMP: There was a young man with a drift of mountain ewes, and he running after them this way and that.

NORA (*With a half-smile*): Far down, stranger?

TRAMP: A piece only.

(*She fills the kettle and puts it on the fire.*)

NORA: Maybe, if you're not easy afeard, you'd stay here a short while alone with himself?

TRAMP: I would surely. A man that's dead can do no hurt.

NORA (*Speaking with a sort of constraint*): I'm going a little back to the west, stranger, for himself would go there one night and another, and whistle at that place, and then the young man you're after seeing – a kind of farmer has come up from the sea to live in a cottage beyond – would walk round to see if there was a thing we'd have to be done, and I'm wanting him this night, the way he can go down into the glen when the sun goes up and tell the people that himself is dead.

TRAMP (*Looking at the body in the sheet*): It's myself will go for him, lady of the house, and let you not be destroying yourself with the great rain.

NORA: You wouldn't find your way, stranger, for there's a small path only, and it running up between two sluigs where an ass and cart would be drowned. (*She puts a shawl over her head.*) Let you be making yourself easy, and saying a prayer for his soul, and it's not long I'll be coming again.

TRAMP (*Moving uneasily*): Maybe if you'd a piece of a grey thread and a sharp needle – there's great safety in a needle, lady of the house – I'd be putting a little stitch here and there in my old coat, the time I'll be praying for his soul, and it going up naked to the saints of God.

NORA (*Takes a needle and thread from the front of her dress and gives it to him.*) There's the needle, stranger, and I'm thinking you won't be lonesome, and you used to the back hills, for isn't a dead man itself more company than to be sitting alone, and hearing the winds crying, and you not knowing on what thing your mind would stay?

TRAMP (*Slowly*): It's true, surely, and the Lord have mercy on us all!

(*NORA goes out. The TRAMP begins stitching one of the tags in his coat, saying the 'De Profundis' under his breath. In an instant the sheet is drawn slowly down, and DAN BURKE looks out. The TRAMP moves uneasily, then looks up, and springs to his feet with a movement of terror.*)

DAN (*With a hoarse voice*): Don't be afeard, stranger; a man that's dead can do no hurt.

TRAMP (*Trembling*): I meant no harm, your honour; and won't you leave me easy to be saying a little prayer for your soul?

(*A long whistle is heard outside.*)

DAN (*Listening, sitting up in his bed and speaking fiercely.*): Ah, the devil mend her... Do you hear that, stranger? Did ever you hear another woman could whistle the like of that with two fingers in her mouth? (*He looks at the table hurriedly.*) I'm destroyed with the drouth, and let you bring me a drop quickly before herself will come back.

TRAMP (*Doubtfully*): Is it not dead you are?

DAN: How would I be dead, and I as dry as a baked bone, stranger?

TRAMP (*Pouring out the whiskey*): What will herself say if she smells the stuff on you, for I'm thinking it's not for nothing you're letting on to be dead?

DAN: It is not, stranger, but she won't be coming near me at all, and it's not long now I'll be letting on, for I've cramp in my back, and my hip's asleep on

me, and there's been the devil's own fly itching my
nose... It's near dead I was wanting to sneeze, and
you blathering about the rain, and Darcy (*bitterly*)
– the devil choke him – and the towering church.
(*Crying out impatiently.*) Give me that whiskey.
Would you have herself come back before I taste a
drop at all?

(*TRAMP gives him the glass and he drinks.*)

... Go over now to that cupboard, and bring me
a black stick you'll see in the west corner by the
wall.

TRAMP (*Taking a stick from the cupboard*): Is that it?

DAN: It is, stranger; it's a long time I'm keeping that
stick, for I've a bad wife in the house.

TRAMP (*With a queer look*): Is it herself, master of the
house, and she a grand woman to talk?

DAN: It's herself, surely, it's a bad wife she is – a bad
wife for an old man, and I'm getting cold, God
help me, though I've an arm to me still. (*He takes
the stick in his hand.*) Let you wait now a short while,
and it's a great sight you'll see in this room in two
hours or three. (*He stops to listen.*) Is that somebody
above?

TRAMP (*Listening*): There's a voice speaking on the
path.

DAN: Put that stick here in the bed, and smooth the
sheet the way it was lying. (*He covers himself up
hastily.*) Be falling to sleep now and don't let on you
know anything, or I'll be having your life.

I wouldn't have told you at all but it's destroyed with the drouth I was.

TRAMP (*Covering his head*): Have no fear, master of the house. What is it I know of the like of you that I'd be saying a word or putting out my hand to stay you at all?

(*He goes back to the fire, sits down on a stool with his back to the bed and goes on stitching his coat.*)

DAN (*Under the sheet, querulously*): Stranger.

TRAMP (*Quickly*): Whisht, whisht. Be quiet I'm telling you, they're coming now at the door.

(*NORA comes in with MICHAEL DARA, a tall, innocent young man, behind her.*)

NORA: I wasn't long at all, stranger, for I met himself on the path.

TRAMP: You were middling long, lady of the house.

NORA: There was no sign from himself?

TRAMP: No sign at all, lady of the house.

NORA (*To MICHAEL*): Go over now and pull down the sheet, and look on himself, Michael Dara, and you'll see it's the truth I'm telling you.

MICHAEL: I will not, Nora, I do be afeard of the dead.

(*He sits down on a stool next the table facing The TRAMP. NORA puts the kettle on a lower hook of the pot-hooks, and piles turf under it.*)

NORA (*Turning to TRAMP*): Will you drink a sup of tea with myself and the young man, stranger, or (*Speaking more persuasively*) will you go into the little room and stretch yourself a short while on the bed. I'm thinking it's destroyed you are walking the length of that way in the great rain.

TRAMP: Is it go way and leave you, and you having a wake, lady of the house? I will not surely. (*He takes a drink from his glass which he has beside him.*) And it's none of your tea I'm asking either. (*He goes on stitching.*)

(*NORA makes the tea.*)

MICHAEL (*After looking at the TRAMP rather scornfully for a moment*): That's a poor coat you have, God help you, and I'm thinking it's a poor tailor you are with it.

TRAMP (*Looks up at him for a moment*): If it's a poor tailor I am, I'm thinking it's poor herd does be running back and forward after a little handful of ewes the way I see yourself running this day, young fellow, and you coming from the fair.

NORA (*Comes back to the table. To MICHAEL in a low voice*): Let you not mind him at all, Michael Dara. He has a drop taken, and it's soon he'll be falling asleep.

MICHAEL: Its no lie he's telling. I was destroyed surely... They were that wilful they were running off into one man's bit of oats, and another man's bit of hay, and tumbling into the red bogs till it's more like a pack of old goats than sheep they

were... Mountain ewes is a queer breed, Nora
Burke, and I'm not used to them at all.

NORA (*Settling the tea things*): There's no one can
drive a mountain ewe but the men do be reared in
the Glen Malure, I've heard them say, and above
by Rathvanna, and the Glen Imaal, men the like of
Patch Darcy, God spare his soul, who would walk
through five hundred sheep and miss one of them,
and he not reckoning them at all.

MICHAEL (*Uneasily*): Is it the man went queer in his
head the year that's gone?

NORA: It is surely.

TRAMP (*Plaintively*): That was a great man, young
fellow, a great man I'm telling you. There was
never a lamb from his own ewes he wouldn't know
before it was marked, and he'd run from this to the
city of Dublin, and never catch for his breath.

NORA (*Turning round quickly*): He was a great man
surely, stranger, and isn't it a grand thing when you
hear a living man saying a good word of a dead
man, and he mad dying?

TRAMP: It's the truth I'm saying, God spare his soul.

(*He puts the needle under the collar of his coat, and
settles himself to sleep in the chimney-corner. NORA sits
down at the table: their backs are turned to the bed.*)

MICHAEL (*Looking at her with a queer look*): I heard
tell this day, Nora Burke, that it was on the path
below Patch Darcy would be passing up and

passing down, and I heard them say he'd never pass it night or morning without speaking with yourself.

NORA (*In a low voice*): It was no lie you heard, Michael Dara.

MICHAEL (*As before*): I'm thinking it's a power of men you're after knowing if it's in a lonesome place you live itself.

NORA (*Slowly, giving him his tea*): It's in a lonesome place you do have to be talking with someone, and looking for someone, in the evening of the day, and if it's a power of men I'm after knowing they were fine men, for I was a hard child to please, and a hard girl to please (*she looks at him a little sternly*), and it's a hard woman I am to please this day, Michael Dara, and it's no lie, I'm telling you.

MICHAEL (*Looking over to see that the TRAMP is asleep and then, pointing to the dead man*): Was it a hard woman to please you were when you took himself for your man?

NORA: What way would I live and I an old woman if I didn't marry a man with a bit of a farm, and cows on it, and sheep on the back hills?

MICHAEL (*Considering*): That's true, Nora, and maybe it's no fool you were, for there's good grazing on it, if it is a lonesome place, and I'm thinking it's a good sum he's left behind.

NORA (*Taking the stocking with money from her pocket, and putting it on the table*): I do be thinking in the

long nights it was a big fool I was that time,
Michael Dara, for what good is a bit of a farm with
cows on it, and sheep on the back hills, when you
do be sitting, looking out from a door the like of
that door, and seeing nothing but the mists rolling
down the bog, and the mists again, and they rolling
up the bog, and hearing nothing but the wind
crying out in the bits of broken trees were left from
the great storm, and the streams roaring with the
rain?

MICHAEL (*Looking at her uneasily*): What is it ails you
this night, Nora Burke? I've heard tell it's the like
of that talk you do hear from men, and they after
being a great while on the back hills.

NORA (*Putting out the money on the table*): It's a bad
night, and a wild night, Michael Dara, and isn't it a
great while I am at the foot of the back hills, sitting
up here boiling food for himself, and food for the
brood sow, and baking a cake when the night falls?

(*She puts up the money, listlessly, in little piles on the
table.*)

Isn't it a long while I am sitting here in the
winter, and the summer, and the fine spring,
with the young growing behind me and the old
passing, saying to myself one time, to look on
Mary Brien who wasn't that height (*Holding out
her hand*), and I a fine girl growing up, and
there she is now with two children, and another
coming on her in three months or four. (*She
pauses.*)

MICHAEL (*Moving over three of the piles*): That's three
pounds we have now, Nora Burke.

NORA (*Continuing in the same voice*): And saying to myself another time, to look on Peggy Cavanagh, who had the lightest hand at milking a cow that wouldn't be easy, or turning a cake, and there she is now walking round on the roads, or sitting in a dirty old house, with no teeth in her mouth, and no sense, and no more hair than you'd see on a bit of a hill and they after burning the furze from it. (*She pauses again.*)

MICHAEL: That's five pounds and ten notes, a good sum, surely!... It's not that way you'll be talking when you marry a young man, Nora Burke, and they were saying in the fair my lambs were the best lambs, and I got a grand price, for I'm no fool now at making a bargain when my lambs are good.

NORA: What was it you got?

MICHAEL: Twenty pound for the lot, Nora Burke... We'd do right to wait now till himself will be quiet a while in the Seven Churches, and then you'll marry me in the chapel of Rathvanna, and I'll bring the sheep up on the bit of a hill you have on the back mountain, and we won't have anything we'd be afeard to let our minds on when the mist is down.

NORA (*Pouring him out some whiskey*): Why would I marry you, Mike Dara? You'll be getting old, and I'll be getting old, and in a little while, I'm telling you, you'll be sitting up in your bed – the way himself was sitting – with a shake in your face, and your teeth falling, and the white hair sticking out round you like an old bush where sheep do be leaping a gap.

(DAN BURKE *sits up noiselessly from under the sheet, with his hand to his face. His white hair is sticking out round his head.*)

NORA (*Goes on slowly without hearing him*): It's a pitiful thing to be getting old, but it's a queer thing surely... It's a queer thing to see an old man sitting up there in his bed, with no teeth in him, and a rough word in his mouth, and his chin the way it would take the bark from the edge of an oak board you'd have building a door... God forgive me, Michael Dara, we'll all be getting old, but it's a queer thing surely.

MICHAEL: It's too lonesome you are from living a long time with an old man, Nora, and you're talking again like a herd that would be coming down from the thick mist (*He puts his arm round her*), but it's a fine life you'll have now with a young man, a fine life surely...

(DAN *sneezes violently. MICHAEL tries to get to the door, but before he can do so, DAN jumps out of the bed in queer white clothes, with the stick in his hand, and goes over and puts his back against it.*)

MICHAEL: The Son of God deliver us... (*Crosses himself and goes backward across the room.*)

DAN (*Holding up his hand at him*): Now you'll not marry her the time I'm rotting below in the Seven Churches, and you'll see the thing I'll give you will follow you on the back mountains when the wind is high.

MICHAEL (*To NORA*): Get me out of it, Nora, for the love of God. He always did what you bid him, and I'm thinking he would do it now.

NORA (*looking at the TRAMP*): Is it dead he is or living?

DAN (*Turning towards her*): It's little you care if it's dead or living I am, but there'll be an end now of your fine times, and all the talk you have of young men and old men, and of the mist coming up or going down. (*He opens the door.*) You'll walk out now from that door, Nora Burke, and it's not tomorrow, or the next day, or any day of your life, that you'll put in your foot through it again.

TRAMP (*Standing up*): It's a hard thing you're saying, for an old man, master of the house, and what would the like of her do if you put her out on the roads?

DAN: Let her walk round the like of Peggy Cavanagh below, and be begging money at the cross roads, or selling songs to the men. (*To NORA.*) Walk out now, Nora Burke, and it's soon you'll be getting old with that life, I'm telling you; it's soon your teeth'll be falling and your head'll be the like of a bush where sheep do be leaping a gap.

(*He pauses; she looks round at MICHAEL.*)

MICHAEL (*Timidly*): There's a fine Union below in Rathdrum.

DAN: The like of her would never go there... It's lonesome roads she'll be going, and hiding herself away till the end will come, and they find her stretched like a dead sheep with the frost on her, or the big spiders, maybe, and they putting their webs on her, in the butt of a ditch.

NORA (*Angrily*): What way will yourself be that day, Daniel Burke? What way will you be that day and you lying down a long while in your grave? For it's bad you are living, and it's bad you'll be when you're dead.

(*She looks at him a moment fiercely, then half turns away and speaks plaintively again.*)

Yet, if it is itself, Daniel Burke, who can help it at all, and let you be getting up into your bed, and not be taking your death with the wind blowing on you, and the rain with it, and you half in your skin.

DAN: It's proud and happy you'd be if I was getting my death the day I was shut of yourself. (*Pointing to the door.*) Let you walk out through that door, I'm telling you, and let you not be passing this way if it's hungry you are, or wanting a bed.

TRAMP (*Pointing to MICHAEL*): Maybe himself would take her.

NORA: What would he do with me now?

TRAMP: Give you the half of a dry bed, and good food in your mouth.

DAN: Is it a fool you think him, stranger, or is it a fool you were born yourself? Let her walk out of that door, and let you go along with her stranger – if it's raining itself – for it's too much talk you have surely.

TRAMP (*Going over to NORA*): We'll be going now, lady of the house – the rain is falling but the air is kind, and maybe it'll be a grand morning by the grace of God.

NORA: What good is a grand morning when I'm destroyed surely, and I going out to get my death walking the roads?

TRAMP: You'll not be getting your death with myself, lady of the house, and I knowing all the ways a man can put food in his mouth... We'll be going now, I'm telling you, and the time you'll be feeling the cold and the frost, and the great rain, and the sun again, and the south wind blowing in the glens, you'll not be sitting up on a wet ditch the way you're after sitting in this place, making yourself old with looking on each day and it passing you by. You'll be saying one time, "It's a grand evening by the grace of God," and another time, "It's a wild night, God help us, but it'll pass surely." You'll be saying –

DAN (*Goes over to them crying out impatiently.*): Go out of that door, I'm telling you, and do your blathering below in the glen.

(*NORA gathers a few things into her shawl.*)

TRAMP (*At the door*): Come along with me now, lady of the house, and it's not my blather you'll be hearing only, but you'll be hearing the herons crying out over the black lakes, and you'll be hearing the grouse, and the owls with them, and the larks and the big thrushes when the days are warm, and it's not from the like of them you'll be hearing a talk of getting old like Peggy Cavanagh, and losing the hair off you, and the light of your eyes, but it's fine songs you'll be hearing when the sun goes up, and there'll be no old fellow wheezing the like of a sick sheep close to your ear.

NORA: I'm thinking it's myself will be wheezing that time with lying down under the Heavens when the night is cold, but you've a fine bit of talk, stranger, and it's with yourself I'll go. (*She goes towards the door, then turns to DAN.*) You think it's a grand thing you're after doing with your letting on to be dead, but what is it at all? What way would a woman live in a lonesome place the like of this place, and she not making a talk with the men passing? And what way will yourself live from this day, with none to care you? What is it you'll have now but a black life, Daniel Burke, and it's not long, I'm telling you, till you'll be lying again under that sheet, and you dead surely.

(*She goes out with the TRAMP. MICHAEL is slinking after them, but DAN stops him.*)

DAN: Sit down now and take a little taste of the stuff, Michael Dara, there's a great drouth on me, and the night is young.

MICHAEL: (*Coming back to the table*). And it's very dry I am surely, with the fear of death you put on me, and I after driving mountain ewes since the turn of the day.

DAN (*Throwing away his stick*): I was thinking to strike you, Michael Dara, but you're a quiet man, God help you, and I don't mind you at all. (*He pours out two glasses of whiskey, and gives one to MICHAEL.*)

DAN: Your good health, Michael Dara.

MICHAEL: God reward you, Daniel Burke, and may you have a long life and a quiet life, and good health with it. (*They drink.*)

CURTAIN

PURGATORY

by W. B. Yeats

PERSONS IN THE PLAY

A Boy

An Old Man

SCENE

A ruined house and a bare tree in the background.

BOY: Half-door, hall door,
    Hither and thither day and night,
    Hill or hollow, shouldering this pack
    Hearing you talk.

OLD MAN: Study that house.
    I think about its jokes and stories;
    I try to remember what the butler
    Said to a drunken gamekeeper
    In mid-October, but I cannot.
    If I cannot, none living can.
    Where are the jokes and stories of a house,
    Its threshold gone to patch a pig-sty?

BOY: So you have come this path before?

OLD MAN: The moonlight falls upon the path,
    The shadow of a cloud upon the house,
    And that's symbolical; study that tree,
    What is it like?

BOY: A silly old man.

OLD MAN: It s like – no matter what it's like.
    I saw it a year ago stripped bare as now,
    So I chose a better trade.
    I saw it fifty years ago
    Before the thunderbolt had riven it,
    Green leaves, ripe leaves, leaves thick as butter,
    Fat, greasy life. Stand there and look,
    Because there is somebody in that house.

(The BOY puts down pack and stands in the doorway.)

BOY: There's nobody here.

OLD MAN: There's somebody there.

BOY: The floor is gone, the windows gone,
    And where there should be roof there's sky,
    And here's a bit of an egg-shell thrown
    Out of a jackdaw's nest.

OLD MAN: But there are some
    That do not care what's gone, what's left:
    The souls in Purgatory that come back
    To habitations and familiar spots.

BOY: Your wits are out again.

OLD MAN: Re-live
    Their transgressions, and that not once
    But many times; they know at last
    The consequence of those transgressions
    Whether upon others or upon themselves;
    Upon others, others may bring help,
    For when the consequence is at an end
    The dream must end; if upon themselves,
    There is no help but in themselves
    And in the mercy of God.

BOY: I have had enough!
    Talk to the jackdaws, if talk you must.

OLD MAN: Stop! Sit there upon that stone.
    That is the house where I was born.

BOY: The big old house that was burnt down?

OLD MAN: My mother that was your grand-dam
    owned it,

This scenery and this countryside,
Kennel and stable, horse and hound –
She had a horse at the Curragh, and there met
My father, a groom in a training stable,
Looked at him and married him.
Her mother never spoke to her again,
And she did right.

BOY: My grand-dad got the girl and the money.

OLD MAN: Looked at him and married him,
And he squandered everything she had.
She never knew the worst, because
She died in giving birth to me,
But now she knows it all, being dead.
Great people lived and died in this house;
Magistrates, colonels, members of Parliament,
Captains and Governors, and long ago
Men that had fought at Aughrim and the Boyne.
Some that had gone on Government work
To London or to India came home to die,
Or came from London every spring
To look at the may-blossom in the park.
They had loved the trees that he cut down
To pay what he had lost at cards
Or spent on horses, drink and women;
Had loved the house, had loved all
The intricate passages of the house,
But he killed the house; to kill a house
Where great men grew up, married, died,
I here declare a capital offence.

BOY: My God, but you had luck! Grand clothes,
And maybe a grand horse to ride.

OLD MAN: That he might keep me upon his level
He never sent me to school, but some

Half-loved me for my half of her:
A gamekeeper's wife taught me to read,
A Catholic curate taught me Latin.
There were old books and books made fine
By eighteenth-century French binding, books
Modern and ancient, books by the ton.

BOY: What education have you given me?

OLD MAN: I gave the education that befits
    A bastard that a pedlar got
    Upon a tinker's daughter in a ditch.
    When I had come to sixteen years old
    My father burned down the house when drunk.

BOY: But that is my age, sixteen years old,
    At the Puck Fair.

OLD MAN: And everything was burnt;
    Books, library, all were burnt.

BOY: Is what I have heard upon the road the truth,
    That you killed him in the burning house?

OLD MAN: There's nobody here but our two selves?

BOY: Nobody, Father.

OLD MAN: I stuck him with a knife,
    That knife that cuts my dinner now,
    And after that I left him in the fire.
    They dragged him out, somebody saw
    The knife-wound but could not be certain
    Because the body was all black and charred.
    Then some that were his drunken friends
    Swore they would put me upon trial,

Spoke of quarrels, a threat I had made.
The gamekeeper gave me some old clothes,
I ran away, worked here and there
Till I became a pedlar on the roads,
No good trade, but good enough
Because I am my father's son,
Because of what I did or may do.
Listen to the hoof-beats! Listen, listen!

BOY: I cannot hear a sound.

OLD MAN: Beat! Beat!
This night is the anniversary
Of my mother's wedding night,
Or of the night wherein I was begotten.
My father is riding from the public-house,
A whiskey-bottle under his arm.

(*A window is lit showing a young girl.*)

Look at the window; she stands there
Listening, the servants are all in bed,
She is alone, he has stayed late
Bragging and drinking in the public-house.

BOY: There's nothing but an empty gap in the wall.
You have made it up. No, you are mad!
You are getting madder every day.

OLD MAN: It's louder now because he rides
Upon a gravelled avenue
All grass to-day. The hoof-beat stops,
He has gone to the other side of the house,
Gone to the stable, put the horse up.
She has gone down to open the door.
This night she is no better than her man
And does not mind that he is half drunk,

She is mad about him. They mount the stairs.
She brings him into her own chamber.
And that is the marriage-chamber now.
The window is dimly lit again.

Do not let him touch you! It is not true
That drunken men cannot beget,
And if he touch he much beget
And you must bear his murderer.
Deaf! Both deaf! If I should throw
A stick or a stone they would not hear;
And that's a proof my wits are out.
But there's a problem: she must live
Through everything in exact detail,
Driven to it by remorse, and yet
Can she renew the sexual act
And find no pleasure in it, and if not,
If pleasure and remorse must both be there,
Which is the greater?
                    I lack schooling.
Go fetch Tertullian; he and I
Will ravel all that problem out
Whilst those two lie upon the mattress
Begetting me.
                    Come back! Come back!
And so you thought to slip away,
My bag of money between your fingers,
And that I could not talk and see!
You have been rummaging in the pack.

(*The light in the window has faded out.*)

BOY: You never gave me my right share.

OLD MAN: And had I given it, young as you are,
    You would have spent it upon drink.

BOY: What if I did? I had a right
　　To get it and spend it as I chose.

OLD MAN: Give me that bag and no more words.

BOY: I will not.

OLD MAN: I will break your fingers.

　　(*They struggle for the bag. In the struggle it drops,*
　　scattering the money. The OLD MAN staggers but does
　　not fall. They stand looking at each other. The window
　　is lit up. A man is seen pouring whiskey into a glass.)

BOY: What if I killed you? You killed my grand-dad,
　　Because you were young and he was old.
　　Now I am young and you are old.

OLD MAN: (*Staring at the window*) Better-looking,
　　those sixteen years –

BOY: What are you muttering?

OLD MAN: 　　　　　　　　　　Younger – and yet
　　She should have known he was not her kind.

BOY: What are you saying? Out with it!

　　(*Old Man points to window.*)

　　My God! The window is lit up
　　And somebody stands there, although
　　The floorboards are all burnt away.

OLD MAN: The window is lit up because my father
　　Has come to find a glass for his whiskey.
　　He leans there like some tired beast.

BOY: A dead, living, murdered man!

OLD MAN: "Then the bride-sleep fell upon Adam":
Where did I read those words?

And yet
There's nothing leaning in the window
But the impression upon my mother's mind;
Being dead she is alone in her remorse.

BOY: A body that was a bundle of old bones
Before I was born. Horrible! Horrible!

(*He covers his eyes.*)

OLD MAN: That beast there would know nothing
being nothing,
If I should kill a man under the window
He would not even turn his head.

(*He stabs the boy.*)

My father and my son on the same jack-knife!
That finishes − there − there − there −

(*He stabs again and again. The window grows dark.*)

"Hush-a-bye baby, thy father's a knight,
Thy mother a lady, lovely and bright."
No, that is something that I read in a book,
And if I sing it must be to my mother,
And I lack rhyme.

(*The stage has grown dark except where the tree stands
in the white light.*)

Study that tree.
It stands there like a purified soul,
All cold, sweet, glistening light.
Dear mother, the window is dark again,
But you are in the light because

I finished all that consequence.
I killed that lad because had he grown up
he would have struck a woman's fancy,
Begot, and passed pollution on.
I am a wretched foul old man
And therefore harmless. When I have struck
This old jack-knife into a sod
And pulled it out all bright again,
And picked up all the money that he dropped,
I'll to a distant place, and there
Tell my old jokes among new men.

(*He cleans the knife and begins to pick up the money.*)

Hoof-beats! Dear God,
How quickly it returns – beat – beat – !

Her mind cannot hold up that dream
Twice a murderer and all for nothing,
And she must animate that dead night
Not once but many times!
              Oh God,
Release my mother's soul from its dream!
Mankind can do no more. Appease
The misery of the living and remorse of the
dead.

THE END